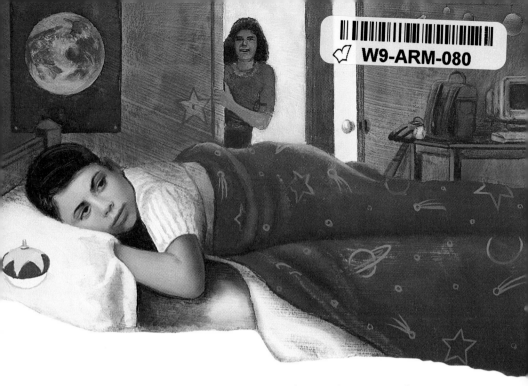

"Well," Leo said slowly, "if she knows about stars and stuff, I guess a week will be okay. Do you think Nana will like being with me?"

"Nana loves you. She wants you to come see her. You'll have a good time together."

"Yeah, but what will I do without cable TV and a computer and the Internet?"

His mother laughed. "I think Nana has planned lots of things for you to do. She tells good stories, too. Now turn off your lamp and go to bed," she said from the doorway to Leo's room. "You have a train to catch in the morning."

Chapter 2

A Blue Velvet Dress?

"We're here, Leo," said Nana as the dust swirled around her battered Jeep. This is it! Welcome to my house."

Leo stepped slowly out of the jeep and looked around. Nana really did live way out in the desert. Her yard had no grass and no trees. There was nothing but cactus and rocks and miles of flat sheets of sandy dirt. No houses nearby. No other kids. Nana's house had a nice deck, but it was much too hot to sit outside. Already Leo could feel the sweat dripping down the side of his face.

"Come on, young man! I want you to get unpacked before dinner!" Nana called to him from the deck.

Leo sighed heavily. He could tell it was going to be a long week.

Nana showed Leo the guest room, and Leo unpacked his clothes. Then he reached deep down in the bottom of his backpack for his toy lion. The gold cloth of its body was rather grubby-looking, and the mane fur was clumped and fuzzy, but Leo didn't care. He'd had the lion forever. He stuffed it under a pillow on the bed, out of sight. He didn't want Nana to think he was a baby.

There was one more thing in the backpack. Mom had given him a special notebook. "This is for you to write about your week so you can remember all the things that you do with Nana," she told him.

On the first page of the notebook, Leo wrote, "Arizona is hot. There's nothing to do. I want to go home."

After dinner he wanted to watch TV. But Nana said, "Come sit with me outside. It's cool in the evening. The breeze is nice."

Leo shrugged his shoulders. "Okay," he said reluctantly. He followed Nana to the deck. It was different outside, very different from the city, just like Mom said it would be.

"Look up, Leo. Isn't it lovely?"

Leo looked up. The sky was so huge and such a dark blue that he could see thousands of stars twinkling brightly. "Wow! What a sky!" he exclaimed. "So many stars! It looks like the floor at school last winter when I spilled glitter."

"Way out here, Leo, you can see the stars and even some of the planets. There's a story

that says the night sky is really the Night Queen's blue velvet dress. All the things you see in the sky are the beautiful decorations on that dress."

"Night Queen? A blue velvet dress? Decorations? You mean like constellations and stuff? Nana, do you know about constellations?"

"I know lots of things," said Nana with a twinkle in her eye. "Let me tell you a bit about the Night Queen. It's an old, old story I heard when I was your age. Maybe someday you'll tell it to someone else."

Leo sat down close to Nana and began to listen.

Chapter 3

The Night Queen

"The Night Queen," Nana began, "lived long, long ago. She was married to a good king. The king loved to gaze up at the night sky. Every night he stared up at it for hours. He loved to look at the moon and the stars. He knew where all of the constellations are, and he knew the name of each one. He watched for meteors and comets in the night sky.

"One day the king became ill. It started with a fever. Then he became pale and thin. Day after day he lay quiet and still in his huge bed. He could not meet with his advisors. He couldn't go on walks among his people, either. Worst of all, he couldn't walk out to look at the night sky. The queen, as you can imagine, was deeply worried.

"Doctors and wise men came from all over
the kingdom. The queen asked the cooks to make
special food for the king. She read to him from
his favorite books. She sang his favorite songs.
His dearest friend, Restor, who often sailed to
faraway lands, came to see him. Nothing seemed
to help.

"One day the queen wore a beautiful, deep
blue velvet dress. 'I like that dress,' the king told
her. 'It reminds me of the night sky. I miss the
night sky,' he said sadly.

"The queen said to herself, *I must find a way
to bring the night sky to him. Perhaps then he
will get better.*"

"That's crazy," said Leo. "How could she bring the whole sky to him?"

Nana smiled. Then she yawned.

"Come on, Nana, what happened?"

"This is a long story, Leo. Tell you what. Each night this week, I'll tell you a little more about the Night Queen's blue velvet dress. Now it's time for bed. We have lots to do this week. You need your rest."

Leo protested, "I'm not tired. Please go on with the story."

Nana said, "Sorry, Leo. I am tired, and I need my rest." And she led Leo inside and kissed him goodnight.

Leo put on his pajamas, brushed his teeth, and climbed into bed. From where he lay, he could look out the window and see the starry sky. He thought about Nana, the Night Queen, and the king. He wondered why the queen was called the Night Queen. *Mom was right*, he thought. *Nana sure can tell good stories. Maybe this week won't be so bad after all.*

Thinking about his mom reminded Leo to write in his notebook. He got the notebook out of his backpack. He wrote, "The sky in Arizona is filled with stars."

Then Leo reached under the pillow for the toy lion. *I wonder what Nana meant when she said we have lots to do*, he said to himself. *Maybe we'll go to a toy store or an arcade*. Then he fell asleep.

Chapter 4

Moon Phases
and a Cameo Pin

Early the next morning, Leo found out what
Nana meant by "lots to do this week." It didn't
include any toy stores or arcades. Nana showed
him a long list of things she wanted him to help
her with. *This is definitely not a vacation*, he
thought as he spread white gravel in Nana's huge
cactus gardens. *More like a work camp.*

"Not so much in one spot, Leo. We have a
lot of area to cover with the gravel. Spread it
out evenly. You need to put more over there.
And if I were you, I'd watch out for the thorns.
They don't feel good when they're buried in
your fingers."

Nana was the boss. She told Leo just what
to do—exactly what to do, how to do it, and
how not to do it.

By evening Leo was glad to just sit. He was so tired he didn't care if he ever moved again, and he had two sore places on his fingers. Nana was right about the cactus thorns. He sat on the deck and looked at all that he had accomplished that day. The new white gravel he had spread around the cactus plants in the front yard glowed in the soft moonlight.

Leo told Nana, "Your yard looks like the moon. You don't have any grass, just sand and rocks. Your plants look like the kind of plants that would grow on the moon—I mean, if anything could grow on the moon."

Nana said, "Some people think the desert looks empty. But I think it looks peaceful."

"I think it's hot!" said Leo.

They sat quietly and sipped lemonade. The warm desert breeze brushed Leo's face. It felt as soft as his mom's silk scarf.

"Speaking of the moon," said Nana, "look over there. It's coming up."

Leo turned to where she pointed. Sure enough, a big, almost-full moon was coming up over the distant hills. "It's huge!" he exclaimed.

"That's called a gibbous moon—when it's almost totally round. It looks like the pin the Night Queen wore on her blue velvet dress," Nana said.

"You said the queen was going to bring the night sky to the king. How could she do that?" Leo asked.

"Well, the queen was very brave, and she loved the king very much. All she could think about was making him well. She believed that she could do anything if she wanted to badly enough. She was determined to bring the night sky inside."

Nana set her lemonade glass down and continued in a low voice. "Here is how she began. When the king had fallen asleep one night, the queen slipped quietly out of the palace. She wore her velvet dress that was exactly the color of the night sky.

The moon was like the one we have tonight. The queen waited and watched. Finally, in the wee hours of the night, she saw that the moon was caught in the branches of a tree. Then she snatched it and hurried back to the castle."

"How did the moon get caught in a tree?" asked Leo.

"It just did. This is a story. Anything can happen in a story."

"Right," said Leo, with a grin. "I knew that."

"Well, the queen looked at the moon in her hand and decided to make the moon into a pin. She put the pin on her dress, right below the neckline."

"The lady on your pin is white like the moon, Nana," Leo said.

"Yes, you're right!" Nana exclaimed. She twisted her blouse around so that Leo could see the woman's face carved against a dark background. "This kind of pin is called a cameo. This one belonged to my mother. We don't know who the lady on it is. Maybe it's a picture of the Night Queen."

"But the Night Queen's pin really was the moon, right?" asked Leo. "The phases of the moon change. Did her pin change?"

"Yes, her pin did change. Sometimes it was dark like a new moon. At other times it looked like a half moon. Sometimes it looked like a full moon," Nana answered.

"I know what all those phases are," said Leo. "At school we've been learning about the moon and why it has phases."

"That's good," said Nana. "Tell me what you have learned."

Leo wrinkled his brow as he tried to remember what his science book said. "Okay, here goes. See, the moon goes around the earth. But the earth and the moon also go around the sun. When the moon is between the earth and the sun, we can't see the daylight side of the moon, so it looks like the moon isn't there. When the earth is between the moon and the sun, we see the full moon. In between we see part of the moon. It looks like the moon changes shape, but it really doesn't."

"Leo, you are smart," Nana said warmly.

Leo thought this week was turning out to be all right, even if Nana made him work hard. Nana told good stories, and she also listened when he talked.

Before he went to bed, Leo wrote some more in his notebook. "I spread gravel all day. Tonight I told Nana about the phases of the moon. Nana is a good grandmother. She listens to me."

The next morning Leo put the toy lion on top of his pillow. Nana could see the lion. She wouldn't think he was a baby.

Chapter 5

Diamond Constellations

"Brush the paint evenly, Leo. Nice, long brush strokes." Nana was giving directions again. Leo didn't mind painting. It was actually kind of fun. The hard part had been scraping all the old paint off the chairs. That had taken all morning.

"Not too much paint on the brush, Leo. You're dripping. Drag your brush against the edge of the can so that you scrape off all the excess paint."

Boy, could Nana boss!

Leo waited until she took a breath, then asked, "Nana, will you tell more of the story tonight? What happened after the Night Queen stole the moon?"

Nana winked at him. "Tell you what, Leo. If you can keep more paint on the chair than on you, I'll tell you more of the story."

Leo painted all afternoon. Paint covered his hands, arms, legs, shoes, shorts, shirt, face, and hair. The chairs looked great.

That evening Leo and Nana sat outside on two large rocks by the deck because the paint on the chairs was still wet. Leo said, "I love looking at the stars."

"Me, too," said Nana.

"I can't do this at home. Mom and I go to the planetarium to see the sky show, but that's not the same as seeing the real thing."

Nana nodded. "I know. That's why I love living here. Can you see the Big Dipper?"

"Where?" asked Leo.

Nana pointed it out in the sky. "That very bright star in the top left corner of the dipper is called the North Star because it always points north. Long ago, sailors used the North Star to steer by."

"I see it!" cried Leo.

"The Big Dipper is part of the constellation called Ursa Major, or the Great Bear," Nana explained.

"Doesn't look like a bear to
me," replied Leo.

"Now look by the handle of the
Big Dipper," Nana said. "Do you see a *W*?"

"Got it," replied Leo.

"That's Cassiopeia," Nana answered. "Some
people call it the Lady in the Chair." Nana
stood up and pointed west. "Let's find your
constellation. Look near the horizon. See that
bright star? It and the stars around it make up
the constellation Leo. *Leo* means 'lion.'"

Leo followed her finger. There it was—his
very own constellation!

"The constellations are in the story of the Night Queen," said Nana. "Do you want to hear some more of the story?"

"Please," said Leo. "What happened after the queen took the moon? Did the king get better?"

"Well, he did notice the pin. He told her it reminded him of the moon, and I guess that showed he was a little better."

"Didn't anybody notice the moon was gone?"

"Not really. There were cloudy nights and rainstorms. Then came the time when we don't see the moon, so people didn't notice right away. The queen didn't stop with the moon, though. She thought that if the moon made the king a little better, maybe the stars would make him completely well. She took whole constellations and sewed them onto the blue velvet of her dress. They looked like diamonds. Each night the queen chose another constellation until the whole sky was dark."

"How awful for the people," said Leo. His eyelids drooped sleepily. "It must have been really scary at night."

"Yes, it was," Nana
murmured as she scooped
him up and took him
inside to bed.

That night, before
he drifted off to sleep,
Leo wrote in his
notebook, "I painted
chairs. Nana showed
me how to find my
constellation."

Chapter 6

Planet Buttons

The next morning dawned hot, hot, hot. It was too hot to do anything outside, so Leo and Nana worked inside.

"Leo, be sure to get all the dust off the back of that chair. Dust is everywhere. Reach way back behind it."

Nana is a general fighting a war against dirt, and I'm the only soldier, Leo thought to himself. *Do this, wipe that, shine here, polish there*.

When every speck of dust was gone, Nana and Leo spent the rest of the day cleaning out drawers. They tossed out, refolded, stacked, and put back all the stuff in all the drawers. They worked hard all the way to dinner time.

After dinner Nana went to her bedroom and came back with an old jewelry box. "Let's see what's in here. Hmm. Here's the ring with the stone as blue as Earth." Nana held up the ring.

"Nana, Earth is brown," Leo objected.

"The land part of it is," she agreed. "But did you know our planet is mostly ocean? That's why it looks blue if you look at it from out in space."

"You wouldn't think it's mostly ocean when you're out here in the desert," said Leo.

"Oh, I'd forgotten all about this," Nana said. "This bracelet is made just like a chain of little planets. The first one is very small, like Mercury. The next one is a pearl for Venus. The third one is a blue stone a little bigger than the pearl. That's for Earth."

"It's beautiful," said Leo. "Can I see?" Leo and Nana looked at the rest of the bracelet together.

"You know, this jewelry reminds me of the Night Queen and how she stole all of the other planets in our solar system," Nana said. "She worked very hard to get them."

"Why was it so hard to do?" Leo asked.

"You tell me. Think about planets," Nana replied.

Leo scratched his head and thought hard. "Well," he said slowly, "most planets don't reflect very much light, so they would be pretty hard to see."

"That's one reason. Tell me another."

Leo thought again. "Is it because the planets go around the sun at different times? And they move at different speeds?" he asked.

"You're so smart!" Nana exclaimed. "Yes, you are right. I'll bet you would be a good astronomer. Then you could study all about stars and planets."

"What did the Night Queen do with the planets?" Leo asked.

"She made them into buttons and stitched them down the front of her blue velvet gown," Nana explained. "Her favorite was one with many little buttons around it."

"That one was Jupiter, wasn't it?" asked Leo. "I'll bet the little buttons were its moons."

"That's right." Nana smiled. "The Night Queen's blue velvet dress then had a cameo moon pin, diamond constellations, and planet buttons."

"Did seeing the dress help the king get well?" asked Leo.

"Yes, it did. The king got stronger as the queen brought the night sky into his room. But the real sky kept getting darker and darker with each item she took."

That night, in his journal Leo wrote, "We cleaned the whole house. I like Nana's house. I like Nana, too."

Chapter 7

Sequins and an Asteroid Belt

The next day was cooler. Nana and Leo were outside with a stepladder, bucket, sponge, squeegee, spray bottle, and several rolls of paper towels.

"First, you wash the glass with soapy water and a sponge," Nana directed Leo. "Next, you squeegee it off and spray the glass with window cleaner. Then, polish it with clean paper towels."

"Nana, how many windows do you have?" Leo asked.

"Well, let's count them," she replied. "Two windows each in the living room, kitchen, my bedroom, and your room. One window in the bathroom. How many is that?"

"Too many," sighed Leo.

"Look. This trail of soapy water on the window looks like a comet," said Nana.

Leo experimented with soapy water, too. "I think mine is a meteor shower."

"Or maybe the asteroid belt," said Nana.

"You know about the asteroid belt?" questioned Leo.

"Of course I do," said Nana. "And so did the Night Queen. The asteroid belt is between Mars and Jupiter. When the planets were gone, the asteroid belt was easy to see. The Night Queen stitched the asteroids to a ribbon and wore the ribbon with her dress as a shining, sparkling belt."

"Did the king get better?" asked Leo.

"Yes. He was getting much better. He began to sit up, and he started to eat. He admired the dress and said it was just like the night sky.

"The queen was happy that the king was getting better. But she had worried so much about the king that she forgot about all the other people. They had no moon, no stars, no planets— almost no light in the sky at night.

Chapter 8

Shooting Stars

"Is this story going to have a sad ending?" asked Leo.

"Wait and see," said Nana.

That evening, in his notebook Leo wrote, "Today we washed windows. Nana told me more about the Night Queen. I don't want the story to have a sad ending." He lay in his bed and gazed out at the brilliant stars in the desert sky. In the moonlight he could make out the largest cactus garden in the front yard.

Leo smiled to himself when he remembered how strange the desert had seemed when he arrived. Now he knew the desert and his Nana's house would always be a special place to him.

The next night was the last night of Leo's vacation with Nana. They sat on the deck together. "Leo," said Nana, "look at all the work we did this week—the cactus gardens, the chairs, the windows. Thanks for all your help."

"It was work, but it was fun, too," said Leo.

"Look!" Nana shouted. "A shooting star! Quick, Leo. Wish on it."

Leo closed his eyes tight and wished hard.

"You know," said Nana, "shooting stars were the last thing the Night Queen took. She then went to the king and spun around and showed him all the beautiful things from the sky.

"The king said, 'Your dress is truly as beautiful as the night sky. I think, though, that I am well enough to go out on the balcony and look at the real sky again.'

"But when the king looked at the sky, there was only darkness. 'What has happened?' he cried in horror. How will people live without the beauty of the night sky? How will sailors ever find their way home?'

"At that moment, of course, the queen realized what she had done. She had wanted to help the king, and that was a very good thing. But she had not thought about what would happen if she took the things from the night sky, and that was a bad thing. 'What I did, I must undo,' she said.

"She went immediately to her rooms. When she returned to the king, he saw that she wore a plain gray gown. In her arms she carried the blue velvet gown. She rushed out to the balcony. Gathering all her strength, she threw the blue velvet gown high into the clouds. The dress spread out wide and long until it filled the whole sky. The moon, constellations, planets, asteroids, and shooting stars all appeared in their right places."

"Did the king stay well?" asked Leo.

"The king stayed well, and they lived to be very old and very happy. And we know the sky stayed bright with stars because you can see them tonight."

Going Home

Nana stretched and yawned. "Let's go inside. You are leaving tomorrow, and we will have to get an early start. It's time for bed."

But not for sleep yet, Leo thought. He had something important to do.

In his room Leo wrote in his notebook, "Nana and I saw a shooting star. I wished on it." He read all he had written throughout the week. Mom was right. The notebook would help him to always remember this week. Very carefully he tore out the pages he had written on and put them in the bottom of his backpack.

In the morning Leo was sleepy. Nana had to wake him for breakfast. "Are you all packed?" she asked.

"Yes, I think so," Leo answered. He checked his backpack. His lion was there, and so were the pages he had torn from his notebook.

"I have a present for your mother, but I want you to see it before I wrap it." Nana held out a small jewelry box.

"It's the cameo pin," said Leo.

"Yes," said Nana. "My mother gave it to me. Now I'm ready to give it to my daughter."

"Whenever Mom wears the cameo pin, I'll think of the Night Queen," Leo said.

"I have a present for you, too." Nana handed him a long box wrapped in paper that had stars on it.

Leo quickly unwrapped the gift. "I can't believe it!" he cried. "A telescope! Awesome! Now I can see the stars at home. Oh, Nana, I'm going to miss you."

"I'll miss you, too. Come back and visit me soon. Bring your telescope, and we'll really see the night sky."

"I have something for you, Nana," whispered Leo. He handed her a flat package. It was wrapped in paper towels. "I didn't have any wrapping paper," he explained.

Nana unwrapped the towels. Inside was Leo's notebook. The pages were full of writing.

Nana opened the cover. "Oh, my. Oh, Leo." She wiped a tear from her eye. Leo had written down the whole story of the Night Queen.

"Nana, do you know what I wished for on the shooting star last night? I wished I could come back and see you very soon," Leo said with a smile.

"Do you know what?" asked Nana. "That's exactly what I wished for! And that is one wish that I know will come true."